Playing The Clip

The Digital Media Creator's Legal Guide to Fair Use

Matthew B. Harrison

TALKERS Books

"The problem with quotes on the internet is that it is hard to verify their authenticity."
— Abraham Lincoln

Published by TALKERS Books.

Printed in the United States of America.

To my wife, Meghan,
and our son, Oliver.

Contents

COMMON MYTHS

None of these are legal defenses.

IF SOMETHING GOES WRONG

Read This Before You Do Anything Else

IT STARTED WITH AN EMAIL

I can't "Play the Clip"?! How is that even possible? I have edited, commented, transformed and modified it. I have made it better.

I hear what you are saying. You want to use other people's work to make your points sparkle.

Clips.
Images.
Audio.
Video.
Screenshots.
Quotes.

That impulse is normal. Modern media is built on it.

But using someone else's copyrighted work without permission is infringement.

That is because copyright infringement is a **strict liability rule**. A distinction that surprises many creators the first time they encounter it.

The law does not ask why something was copied before it asks whether it was copied.

Intent comes later.
Context comes later.
Justification comes later.

Infringement exists first.

If the term *fair use* is unfamiliar, it refers to the limited circumstances in which copyright law allows someone to quote, reference, or reproduce portions of a protected work without permission.

Not sometimes.
Not morally.
Not theoretically.

Legally.

The doctrine exists so that criticism, commentary, reporting, and analysis can refer to the material they are discussing. Without it, modern speech would collapse under the weight of copyright restrictions.

Most creators resist that sentence immediately and respond with reasons to excuse the copying.

Everyone does it.
I'm commenting on the topic.
I'm criticizing the presentation.
I'm educating people.
It's news.
I gave credit.

It's a short clip.
Who's going to sue me?

None of those responses change the starting point.

They do not determine whether infringement occurred. They matter only when determining harm and damages.

Infringement exists first.

So what is fair use?

It is a legal defense raised **after copying has already happened and been challenged**. Fair use does not prevent infringement from occurring. It does not authorize copying in advance.

That order matters.

Most creators invert it. They start with justification and assume infringement never occurred. Courts do the opposite. They start with copying and then decide whether that copying should be excused.

And that is not a low bar to meet.

This book begins there — not because it is comfortable, but because it is accurate.

INTRODUCTION

FAIR USE IS THE DEFENSIVE JUSTIFICATION FOR COPYRIGHT INFRINGEMENT

Modern media now spans many forms: broadcasting, podcasting, streaming video, social platforms, and on-demand clips. Throughout this book, the term **media creators** refers collectively to the professionals working across those environments, including broadcasters, podcasters, journalists, commentators, and digital creators.

The legal principles discussed here apply to all of them.

In copyright law, "copying" does not mean every act of duplication in the everyday sense. It refers to the reproduction of protected expression in a way that implicates one of the copyright holder's exclusive rights.

Under that framework, copying is the starting condition — not the conclusion. Lawful backups, incidental technical copies, and quotations for purposes such as criticism or commentary may be excused, justified, licensed, or immunized. But analytically, they still involve the reproduction of protected expression. The law asks first whether that reproduction occurred without permission. Only then does it ask whether liability should attach.

Intent, good faith, and giving credit do not matter.

You can infringe while educating, criticizing, and even while reporting the news.

None of those things, alone and in a vacuum, prevent infringement from occurring.

Copyright infringement is strict liability. The law does not ask what you meant to do. It does not ask whether you thought the use was fair. It does not ask whether everyone else was doing the same thing. It asks one question first: was protected expression copied without permission?

If the answer is yes, infringement exists. Everything else comes later.

This is where most creators get turned around.

Good storytelling has always required description. Reporting, commentary, and analysis traditionally involved explaining what happened, recounting what was said, or summarizing events for an audience that was not present.

Media operated the same way. For decades, broadcasters, journalists, and commentators relied on narrative description to convey facts accurately and neutrally to audiences who depended on that information. The storyteller stood in for the moment itself.

That is still true today — but the underlying dynamic has changed. Cameras are everywhere. Audio is always rolling. Courtrooms, interviews, public meetings, performances, and breaking news events are now routinely recorded. In many cases, the original footage — or someone else's coverage of it — already exists and is easily accessible.

Across radio, podcasts, streaming video, social platforms, and on-demand clips, creators increasingly show the thing itself rather than talk around it.

And often, the thing being shown belongs to someone else. It is not raw actuality, and it is not automatically free to use.

At TALKERS magazine, we refer to this cross-platform approach as the "Play the Clip" technique. It includes the use of audio excerpts, video segments, screenshots, quotes, and visual references as core components of commentary, analysis, and storytelling. Playing the Clip allows the material to speak for itself in a fast-paced, attention-fractured media environment.

Fair use does not prevent infringement; nor does it encourage it. It gives those that take the risk a justification that defends that choice. It does not sanitize copying; nor does it operate as permission granted in advance. Fair use is argued only after infringement has already occurred. It is a defensive justification, raised in response to a claim that the law recognizes as valid on its face.

That framing is uncomfortable, but it is essential.

Most confusion about fair use comes from treating it as a right rather than a response. Creators talk about "having" fair use, or "qualifying" for fair use, as though it were something carried into the creative process. Courts do not see it that way. They encounter fair use only after a work has been copied, published, challenged, and reconstructed in hindsight.

Fair use exists to excuse certain infringements, not to authorize copying in advance.

Once that order is clear, the rest of the doctrine begins to make sense.

Why This Matters Immediately

Infringement does not announce itself politely. It shows up operationally.

A takedown notice.

A copyright strike.

Muted audio.

Blocked video.

Lost monetization.

These are not judgments about fairness. They are reactions to copying. Platforms do not evaluate intent or nuance at scale. They act to manage volume, reduce exposure, and protect revenue.

As a result, creators experience copyright enforcement as arbitrary. Massive amounts of copied material remain live. Other material disappears instantly.

Silence feels like approval. Longevity feels like safety.

Neither is true.

Enforcement is not the law. It is a rough, automated response to infringement signals. Courts come later, if they come at all.

That gap — between how infringement is experienced and how fair use is judged — is where misunderstanding thrives.

What Fair Use Actually Is (Stated Plainly)

Fair use is a legal defense.

Fair use is not permission.

It is not a license.

It is not a checklist.

It is not evaluated before infringement, but rather after the fact, based on specific circumstances, by someone who was not present when the creative decision was made. Invoking fair use is not a denial of copying. It is an argument that the copying should be excused.

That is why fair use feels unstable. Creators make decisions forward-facing, under pressure. Courts judge those decisions backward-facing, in slow motion, stripped of context and urgency.

Fair use is not moral; it is functional.

Why Fair Use Exists at All

If copyright law ended with infringement, modern speech would not survive.

Criticism requires reference. Commentary requires quotation. News reporting requires excerpts. Parody requires recognition. Some ideas cannot be discussed meaningfully without pointing to the thing itself.

Fair use exists to preserve that space.

It is the pressure valve in a system that would otherwise choke the very discourse copyright was meant to encourage. It allows limited use of protected expression when that use serves a different function and does not replace the original in the marketplace.

But fair use was never designed to be comfortable. It trades certainty for flexibility. It tolerates risk to preserve speech. It asks courts to weigh judgment rather than apply formulas.

That design choice explains both its necessity and its frustration.

Fair Use Before Anyone Calls It That

Most people rely on fair use long before they ever hear the term.

They quote a movie line to explain why a scene worked.

They screenshot a post to criticize it.

They play a few seconds of audio to explain sound or structure.

These acts feel natural because they mirror how humans communicate. We reference what exists to explain, critique, and recontextualize it. Description often fails where demonstration succeeds.

Fair use reflects that primal gut instinct.

Problems arise when instinct becomes format.

What "Play the Clip" Actually Means

"Play the Clip" is not a slogan; it is a media format. It is not even a format. It is a popular technique used within several formats.

It reflects a belief that showing the thing itself is more accurate than describing it. That audiences want primary material. That credibility is enhanced when people can see or hear the original moment for themselves.

Modern platforms reward this relentlessly. Clips are fast. Clips are legible. Clips minimize friction and maximize engagement.

Creators reach for clips for understandable reasons: precision, speed, clarity, trust.

There is also something deeper at work.

Humans have an inherent drive to take what exists and make it bigger, clearer, louder, more compelling. We remix. We enhance. We amplify. That instinct is ancient. What is new is the scale at which it now operates — and the systems that reward it.

"Play the Clip" sits at the intersection of instinct and incentive.

Chapter One

WHY FAIR USE FEELS BROKEN

Fair use is not broken — but it feels that way.

Creators experience the process as arbitrary, unpredictable, asymmetric, and stacked against them.

Fair use did not become confusing.

The environment around it changed.

The doctrine was built for one set of conditions and now operates inside another. It still asks the same questions, but creators encounter them within platform-driven systems that reward speed, familiarity, and scale over restraint. Expecting fair use to behave the same way under those conditions is a category mistake. The law did not fail. The context shifted.

For most of the twentieth century, media creation happened inside bounded systems. Broadcasts aired at specific times. Audiences were finite. Content disappeared by design. Even when material was recorded, distribution required effort, cost, and intent. Those limits acted as natural governors on risk.

Modern media has none of those constraints.

Content now persists. It can be replayed, clipped, embedded, re-posted, shared, remixed, archived, and monetized indefinitely — often by people far removed from the original act of creation. A decision that once lived for minutes now lives indefinitely. A choice that once affected a local audience can now travel globally — on air and online, live or prerecorded, clipped, cut, edited, re-posted, shared, remixed, or consumed on demand — moving from instinct to publication independent of original intent or context.

Fair use did not evolve at the same pace.

Most modern creators do not learn copyright law from statutes or court opinions. They learn it socially — by observation rather than instruction. They look at what thrives under platform rules, norms, and incentives, and they copy it. What performs well becomes what feels permissible.

That shorthand is powerful — but often wrong.

Platforms reinforce this misunderstanding by design. Algorithms favor content that delivers immediate payoff and minimizes friction — especially friction that sends audiences elsewhere. Clips that feel complete outperform excerpts that redirect. Familiar material outperforms restraint. Reuse that keeps viewers inside the system is rewarded more consistently than originality that sends audiences elsewhere.

At the same time, enforcement is uneven.

Vast amounts of infringing material remain live for years. Some content is removed quickly. Other content flourishes. That inconsistency breeds false confidence. Visibility is mistaken for approval. Endurance is mistaken for legality. In reality, enforcement reflects complaint-driven systems, resource limits, and selective attention — not validation.

Fair use is not shaped by scale or repetition. Courts evaluate it by examining specific facts, not by tallying how often a practice occurs.

Another source of confusion is tone. Fair use discussions often feel academic, abstract, or moralizing. Creators are told what they "should" do without being shown how courts actually think. Others swing in the opposite direction, treating fair use as a magic phrase that excuses anything critical, creative, or popular.

Neither approach works.

Fair use exists to protect important speech — critique, commentary, news reporting, parody, and transformation. It does not exist to excuse convenience, decoration, or substitution. Understanding the difference requires judgment, not slogans.

This book is written for professionals who create in real time, under pressure, inside platform-driven systems that reward speed and familiarity. It assumes intelligence.

It also does not pretend that traditional broadcasters and online creators live in different legal universes.

Regardless of format — on air, online, live, prerecorded, clipped, re-posted, shared, remixed, or on demand — the same civil liability standards apply. The Federal Communications Commission may regulate broadcasters. It does not regulate defamation, copyright infringement, or misrepresentation. Courts do.

What follows is not a checklist of safe uses or a catalog of horror stories. It explains how fair use functions in practice — where creators misread it, where platforms distort it, and where risk accumulates.

Fair use is not broken. The way modern creators experience it almost guarantees misunderstanding.

That is the problem this book tries to solve.

Chapter Two

WHAT FAIR USE ACTUALLY IS

(AND WHAT IT IS NOT)

Fair use is often described as a defense, but that framing obscures how it operates.

Fair use is not a permission slip granted in advance. It is a judgment made after the fact, based on specific circumstances. Courts do not ask whether a creator felt justified, believed they were being fair, or followed industry practice. They ask what happened, why it happened, and what effect it had within the specific facts.

That distinction matters.

Most misunderstandings about fair use stem from the desire for certainty in a doctrine that resists certainty. Creators want rules. Platforms offer guidelines. Commentators provide checklists. None substitute for legal analysis, because fair use does not function mechanically.

Fair use turns on a fact-specific inquiry.

That inquiry is contextual, not categorical. No single factor controls the outcome. No phrase, disclaimer, or label transforms infringement into protection. Courts examine the totality of the circumstances and weigh competing interests rather than apply formulas.

The statute identifies four considerations — purpose, nature, amount, and market effect — but those factors are not boxes to check. They are lenses through which courts evaluate conduct. The same act can be fair in one context and infringing in another, depending on how and why it is used.

Purpose matters, but not in the way creators assume.

Adding commentary, criticism, or humor does not automatically transform a use into fair use. Courts look beyond surface intent to function. The question is not whether the new work adds something, but whether it performs a different function. Transformation is measured by function, not effort.

Nature matters, but it rarely decides the case on its own.

Creative works receive stronger protection than factual ones, but that distinction does not eliminate fair use or guarantee it. Courts consider whether the original work was published, how expressive it is, and how central its creative elements are to the secondary use.

Amount matters, even when the use feels small.

Taking less does not automatically make a use fair. Courts ask whether what was taken was reasonable in relation to the purpose asserted. Using the "heart" or most memorable portion of a work can weigh heavily against fair use, even if the quantity is limited.

Market effect often carries the most weight.

Courts examine whether the secondary use substitutes for the original or harms a legitimate licensing market. This does not require proof of actual lost sales. It requires a showing that the use usurps demand or interferes with how the original creator reasonably exploits the work.

This analysis is practical, not theoretical.

Courts are less concerned with how a creator characterizes the work than with how audiences experience it. If the audience no longer needs the original after consuming the secondary work, the fair use claim weakens. If the secondary use serves as a replacement rather than a reference, the risk increases.

Courts do not evaluate fair use through the lens of intent or virtue. They approach it as an economic and functional inquiry, focused on what the use does rather than how it feels. It does not reward good intentions. It does not punish bad motives. It evaluates consequences. That evaluation happens in hindsight, often long after the original decision to publish was made.

It offers protection without certainty and flexibility without guarantees. It asks creators to exercise judgment in environments that reward speed, familiarity, and replication. It demands restraint without providing bright lines.

But that instability is not a flaw.

Fair use works precisely because it is fact-specific. Each analysis is confined to the particular use, the particular work, and the particular context in which the decision was made. That limitation frustrates anyone looking for rules, but it allows courts to evaluate unique circumstances without distorting them to fit a formula.

That flexibility is intentional. Fair use is designed to adapt, balancing the interests of creators, commentators, journalists, and the public without freezing innovation or speech. It requires courts to look closely at facts rather than rely on abstractions.

The chapters that follow do not replace this analysis. They apply it.

Each chapter takes a common creative act — clipping, reposting, reacting, embedding, using music, generating content with AI — and examines how courts are likely to view it when something goes wrong. The goal is not to make creators timid. It is to make them literate.

Fair use is not a shield you carry.

It is a judgment you invite.

Understanding that difference is the foundation for everything that comes next.

Chapter Three

IDEAS, EXPRESSION, AND THE FIRST BOUNDARY

Ideas are free. Expression is protected.

Copyright law does not protect ideas. Courts do not treat discussion of ideas, by itself, as a copyright claim.

That distinction is the first boundary in understanding fair use. Everything that follows depends on this boundary.

Ideas are concepts, themes, facts, opinions, and general narratives. Expression is the particular way those things are conveyed — the words chosen, the images framed, the sounds arranged, the pacing, structure, and sequence that make a work recognizable as that work and not something else.

Courts return to this boundary because it prevents copyright from swallowing speech.

If ideas themselves were protectable, the first person to express a concept could lock it away indefinitely — a result reserved for patent law, not copyright. Copyright encourages creation without granting ownership over thought itself.

This is where creators misstep.

They assume that because they are discussing an idea — a topic, controversy, or cultural moment — whatever they include must be fair. But the law does not protect discussion in the abstract. It evaluates what was taken, how it was used, and whether the expression itself was necessary to convey the idea.

Talking about a movie is not the same as showing it. Discussing a song is not the same as playing it. Critiquing a performance is not the same as reproducing it.

This is the pressure point for creators who "Play the Clip."

Playing the Clip may be justified when the clip itself is the subject of the critique. It may be defensible when a brief excerpt is necessary to analyze sound, structure, or technique rather than deliver the experience. It may be permissible when the expression is required to illustrate a point and no meaningful substitute exists.

In each case, "Play the Clip" is tolerated only when the clip performs analytical work, not entertainment's work.

The more a creator depends on the original expression to carry the audience's experience, the more the analysis shifts.

This is why summaries and paraphrases often feel safer than direct excerpts. They allow ideas to be conveyed without appropriating expression. That does not make them automatically fair, but it changes the posture of the use.

Courts are sensitive to this distinction because expression is where economic value often resides — and where audience attention tends to concentrate.

Ideas do not substitute. Expression can.

When a secondary use reproduces expressive elements — visuals, dialogue, music, pacing, structure — it begins to overlap with the market for the original. That overlap is what copyright law polices.

Fair use operates inside this boundary.

It asks whether copying protected expression was justified under the circumstances. The idea–expression divide determines what was taken. The factors evaluate whether taking it was permissible.

Creators often collapse these steps. They move from "I am discussing an idea" to "my use must be fair," skipping the threshold question of whether protected expression was necessary at all.

Copyright protection requires only minimal originality. Facts are not protected, but once expression crosses that low threshold, even small portions can be protected — a short clip, a single image, a brief phrase.

Understanding this boundary does not limit creativity. It clarifies it.

Creators are free to engage with ideas, themes, news, criticism, and commentary without permission. They are not free to appropriate expressive choices simply because those choices make the point easier to make.

When courts analyze fair use, they are not asking whether an idea was discussed. They are asking whether protected expression was taken, how it was used, and whether that use displaced the original's function in the marketplace.

The idea–expression divide is not a technicality.

It is the first gate.

Chapter Four

THE LINE BETWEEN IDEAS AND EXPRESSION

The idea–expression dichotomy sounds simple until you apply it in real-world media.

Creators rarely misunderstand the rule itself. They misunderstand its application because modern media collapses the distance between ideas and expression in ways the law refuses to recognize.

Ignorance of the law is no excuse. The resulting confusion is understandable — and often relied upon.

What feels like commentary often relies on expression. What feels like reference often functions as reproduction. What feels harmless can carry the weight of substitution.

Chapter 3 established the boundary: ideas are free; expression is protected.

This chapter addresses what happens in practice. The contrast is clear. The application rarely is.

Copyright regulates conduct, not feeling. That focus is intentional.

The law is not concerned with what a creator meant to communicate. Courts do not evaluate motivation or sincerity. They evaluate precision — what was taken, how it was used, and what role it played for the audience.

Copyright protects expression, not ideas.

Lawyers call this the idea–expression dichotomy. On paper, it looks tidy. In practice, especially in modern media, ideas and expression bleed into each other constantly. Creators experience that bleed as natural, driven by the incentives of reach, speed, and recognition.

The law does not follow those incentives.

Patent law protects inventions and functional solutions. Copyright protects creative expression — the particular arrangement of words, images, sounds, sequences, and edits that communicate something in a specific way. No one can own the idea of a talk radio host interviewing a guest about education. But the particular phrasing, structure, and presentation of that exchange can be protected.

Ideas remain free.

Expression does not.

Copyright focuses on execution rather than meaning because meaning is unstable. Meaning shifts with context, audience, and interpretation. If the law attempted to protect themes or messages, culture would stall. Commentary and reinterpretation would collapse.

So the law protects what is concrete and identifiable: the expressive choices a creator makes.

Words. Images. Sounds. Structure. Editing. Sequence. These are the elements that carry value — and exposure.

Modern media makes this boundary harder to see because it rewards familiarity and speed. A clip gains traction, is reposted, reacted to, remixed, and folded into new content streams. Each iteration feels like participation in new conversation rather than appropriation of expression.

Creativity thrives in that environment. So does confusion — and so does exploitation.

A clip intended to reference an idea can become the thing audiences come for. A moment used to illustrate a point can become the point itself. Virality does not ask whether expression was necessary. Copyright does.

This is where creators get tripped up.

Most people sense the difference intuitively, but copyright law operates on a narrower definition than instinct. Creators often believe they are borrowing an idea when they are borrowing protected expression. That mistake becomes easier as digital tools collapse the distance between reference and reproduction — and easier still in environments where sourcing and authorship are obscured.

The more seamless that collapse becomes, the easier it is to cross the line unnoticed.

This distinction is not academic. It is structural. Fair use analysis depends on it because courts cannot evaluate justification without first identifying what was taken.

Skip this distinction and every later question becomes unmoored.

Understanding where ideas end and expression begins does not answer every fair use question. Ignore it, and every later fair use question starts from the wrong premise.

Chapter Five

THE MODERN TENSION: MONETIZATION VS PUBLIC ACCESS

Copyright was designed to strike a balance. Today that balance is under constant strain.

Creators want to monetize their work because the alternative is disappearing from the marketplace. Making a living in platform-mediated media has become an endurance test shaped by shifting algorithms, shrinking payouts, and audiences conditioned to expect content instantly and without cost. Platforms want frictionless sharing. Users want unlimited access. Broadcasters and digital creators are left in the middle — relying on existing cultural material to stay relevant while trying to prevent their own work from being absorbed without compensation.

This tension is not abstract. It appears in everyday editorial decisions:

A guest references a story, and Playing the Clip feels easier than asking the audience to follow a link later or search for context elsewhere.

A politician posts a video, and you want to critique it line by line, which effectively requires Playing the Clip.

A meme spreads, and you feel compelled to "Play the Clip" because excluding the audience from the joke undermines the commentary.

A network segment goes viral, and your audience expects immediate commentary, not a summary.

To the public, these exchanges feel like the natural flow of culture. To the copyright holder, they often look like uncompensated use. To the media creator, they feel unavoidable — part of the job rather than a legal choice, even though the law ultimately turns on those editorial decisions.

Modern content circulation resembles a negotiation in which no party leaves satisfied. Creators give up control. Audiences give up clarity about where content originates. Broadcasters and digital creators give up time, money, and legal certainty simply to participate in the conversation.

Technology intensifies every part of this pressure.

Platforms monetize attention, not accuracy. Their systems reward reuse, repetition, reaction, and remix. Content that feels familiar travels farther than content that requires patience. Algorithms favor material that delivers immediate payoff and minimizes friction, especially friction that sends audiences elsewhere. Platforms benefit at every stage: more eyes, more engagement, more profit.

The law has not fully adapted to this environment.

Fair use was built to mediate disputes over quotation, criticism, and commentary in relatively stable markets. One of the most influential fair use cases turned on whether a magazine could publish a portion of Gerald

Ford's autobiography explaining his decision to pardon Richard Nixon. That is the historical pace of legal development. We are now using that same framework to referee an ecosystem built on clips, fragments, and perpetual circulation.

The result is not a clean three-way balance. It is a crowded collision — and it becomes even more convoluted when platform liability enters the picture, particularly as courts continue to wrestle with the scope and limits of Section 230.

Creators want compensation because their livelihoods depend on it, and the economics of creative work are increasingly fragile.

The public wants access — instant, free, and limitless — not out of malice, but because the system trained them to expect it.

Platforms want attention, and every incentive pushes toward frictionless sharing and maximum reuse while insulating themselves from most downstream liability.

Broadcasters and digital creators absorb pressure from all sides. They depend on existing cultural material to do their jobs, even as their own work is redistributed the moment it goes live.

Fair use is often invoked to navigate this tension, but it remains an imprecise tool — applied by different judges, in different federal circuits, under overlapping but not identical interpretive traditions. It does not resolve the conflict. It manages it case by case, after the fact, through fact-specific analysis rather than bright lines.

This is the environment media creators navigate every day.

Until Congress rewrites the statute or courts draw clearer boundaries, creators will continue operating in gray territory. The goal is not to eliminate risk. It is to understand it well enough to manage it, contain it, and where possible shift exposure away from the individual creator and toward systems designed to absorb it.

That is the work ahead.

Chapter Six

WHAT ACTUALLY COUNTS AS INFRINGEMENT

Most creators misunderstand infringement because they incorrectly believe that intent matters.

Intent may matter morally, ethically, or professionally. It may matter to audiences, peers, employers, or editors. It does not matter to the legal classification.

Copyright infringement is a strict liability rule. That phrase sounds academic, but its meaning is brutally practical. You can infringe without trying to. You can infringe while doing journalism. You can infringe while criticizing the original creator. You can infringe while acting in good faith, while helping the public, or while believing you are "doing it right."

None of that is decisive.

The law asks one question first:

Did you use protected expression without permission?

If the answer is yes, you are already in infringement territory. Everything else comes later.

This is where fair use enters the picture, and this is where many creators get the sequence wrong. Fair use does not prevent infringement from occurring. It does not sanitize the act. It does not operate prospectively. Invoking fair use is an admission that copying happened and that permission was not obtained. The argument is not "this wasn't infringement." The argument is "this infringement should be excused."

That distinction matters because it reframes how risk accumulates.

Creators often talk about fair use as if it were a green light, something that authorizes reuse in advance. Courts treat it as a justification offered after the fact. That difference explains why confidence based on habit, platform norms, or industry practice so often collapses when a dispute actually arises.

Infringement is not defined by motive. It is defined by conduct.

The Forms Infringement Takes in Modern Media

In broadcasting and digital creation, infringement rarely looks dramatic.

None of these acts are exotic. All of them are ordinary. That is the problem. It appears in familiar, everyday acts that feel routine precisely because they are embedded in the job.

Playing the Clip

Audio excerpts, video segments, interview clips, news footage, podcast audio, recorded calls, sponsor reels, and music stings are all protected works. If someone else owns the recording, permission is required unless fair use applies.

Reposting Video

Uploading, re-hosting, screen-capturing, or streaming someone else's content, whether from cable news, YouTube, TikTok, or a livestream, is not neutral redistribution. It is copying.

Using Music

Music is the most unforgiving category because it lives inside mature licensing markets. Even short excerpts can trigger exposure. Attribution does not change that. Good intentions do not change that. Background use does not change that.

Images, Memes, and Screenshots

The internet treats images as communal. Copyright law does not. A screenshot is a reproduction. A meme is not exempt simply because it is widely shared.

Each of these acts feels small in isolation. None of them are small legally. What matters is not how often they happen, but whether protected expression was used without permission and whether a defense exists to justify that use.

Fair use is the defense most creators rely on, often without realizing how narrow it actually is.

Why Fair Use Feels Like Permission (and Isn't)

Fair use is the reason modern media functions at all. Without it, criticism, commentary, news reporting, parody, and analysis would be impossible. But its role is corrective, not permissive. It exists to excuse certain uses after infringement has already occurred, not to authorize copying in advance.

This is why courts are unsentimental about it.

Fair use does not care that a use was common, that "everyone does it," or that the creator felt justified. It cares whether the facts line up.

That analysis always begins from the same starting point: copying happened. Permission was not granted. The only remaining question is whether the use was justified under the circumstances.

Creators often reverse that order in their own thinking. They start with purpose, journalism, commentary, critique, and assume that purpose prevents infringement from existing at all. Courts do the opposite. They start with copying and ask whether purpose, amount, and effect excuse it.

Understanding that order changes how risk should be evaluated.

If fair use truly required a full trial every time it was invoked, the court system would be paralyzed.

It is not. And that fact is instructive.

Most fair use disputes never reach a courtroom. They resolve earlier, through demand letters, takedowns, licensing negotiations, or quiet exits. Not because the doctrine is simple, but because outcomes are often predictable to those who understand how courts evaluate risk.

Experienced lawyers do not need certainty to advise clients. They need probability. When a use plainly substitutes for the original, draws from the most valuable expressive elements, or undermines an existing licensing market, the likely trajectory becomes clear long before a judge is involved. At that point, continuing to fight is often more expensive than cutting losses.

Settlement is not an admission of wrongdoing. It is a recognition of exposure.

Creators rarely see this part of the system. They encounter fair use only at the moment of conflict, when positions harden and emotions rise. By then, the quiet risk assessments have already been made. The law has not become vague at that stage. It has become operational.

Understanding infringement as the baseline condition, rather than a moral accusation, explains why so many disputes end without a ruling. Fair use is tested constantly. It is just tested off the record.

Broadcasting Does Not Get a Different Rule

One of the most persistent myths in media is that broadcasting operates under a softer standard. It does not.

Licensed broadcasters face additional regulatory obligations, but copyright law does not bend for them. Playing the Clip on the air is still copying. Re-posting a segment online is still copying. The medium does not change the analysis. The persistence of the use often makes it worse.

Traditional broadcasting felt safer because content faded, not because the rules were different, but because exposure expired. Digital media does not fade. It persists, travels, and compounds. A decision that once lived for minutes now lives indefinitely. That longevity makes market harm easier to argue and substitution easier to prove.

Fair use did not shrink. Exposure expanded.

Infringement Is the Baseline, Not the Failure

Creators often talk about infringement as if it were an accusation reserved for bad actors. That framing is emotionally satisfying but legally useless. Infringement is the baseline condition that triggers analysis, not a moral verdict.

Once you accept that, fair use becomes easier to understand and harder to abuse.

Fair use is not there to save sloppy decisions, to excuse convenience, or to protect redistribution dressed up as commentary.

It exists to protect uses that add something meaningfully new, uses that rely on protected expression only to the extent necessary and do not replace the original's role in the marketplace.

Everything else is exposure.

The chapters that follow examine how courts actually evaluate that exposure. Not in the abstract, but in the specific contexts creators encounter every day: clips, reposting, reaction formats, music, images, and AI-generated content.

Before any of that analysis can make sense, one idea must be clear:

Fair use does not determine whether infringement occurred.

It determines whether infringement is excused.

That is the line most creators cross without realizing it, and the line this guide exists to make visible.

Everything that follows in this guide assumes infringement as the starting point, not the mistake. Once copying is established, courts move to a different question: whether the use can be justified under the framework copyright law provides.

Chapter Seven

REGULATION IS NOT LIABILITY

One of the most persistent misconceptions in media is that regulatory compliance equals safety.

It does not.

Licensed broadcasters operate under real and consequential oversight. The Federal Communications Commission regulates how messages are delivered: time of day, signal reach, audience protection, political broadcasting rules, indecency standards, emergency alerts, and public files. That oversight is real, and it matters. Stations ignore it at their peril.

It governs delivery, not liability.

Civil courts govern liability.

That distinction is structural, not semantic. Misunderstanding it is one of the most common ways media creators misjudge risk.

Regulation Is Not Immunity

The FCC regulates a specific kind of harm: harm to listeners and the public as defined by statute and community standards.

When a station is fined for indecent language during morning drive, that is a harm determination. When political broadcasting rules are enforced, that is a harm determination. When license renewal is conditioned on compliance history, that is a harm determination.

Those determinations are regulatory, not compensatory.

They do not resolve whether someone was defamed, whether copyright was infringed, or whether a guest's conduct created civil exposure. Those questions belong to courts, not agencies.

A broadcaster can comply fully with FCC rules and still defame someone. A host can satisfy indecency standards and still infringe copyright. A station can pass every regulatory test and still lose a lawsuit. Regulatory compliance does not excuse torts. It never has.

Why the Illusion Took Hold

For decades, broadcasters operated in conditions that made this distinction easy to miss.

Content aired at fixed times. Audiences were geographically bounded. Material disappeared unless deliberately preserved. Risk often faded before it matured. When trouble arose, it frequently arrived in the form of regulatory scrutiny rather than litigation.

That history bred a quiet assumption: if the FCC did not intervene, the content must have been acceptable.

That conclusion was never legally sound.

The FCC is one agency with finite resources. Enforcement is complaint-driven, priority-based, and influenced by volume, timing, and politics. Silence does not mean approval. It means the issue did not rise high enough to trigger enforcement.

At various points in talk radio's history, organized groups funded complaint campaigns precisely because the system operated that way. The presence or absence of enforcement often said more about complaint volume and agency capacity than about legal merit.

The law never changed. Distribution did.

FCC for Thee, Liability for All

This mismatch deserves a warning label.

Call it "FCC for Thee, Liability for All."

Broadcasters live under two systems at once. The FCC governs the wrapper: how the message is transmitted.

Civil courts govern the message itself, what was said, what was taken, and what harm followed.

Digital creators experience the opposite: little operational regulation and full exposure to content-based liability. Different regulatory structures. Identical civil standards.

The broadcaster does not get less liability. The online creator does not get more protection. The rules converge at the courthouse door.

Persistence Changed the Stakes

Broadcast once faded. Digital media does not. The difference is decisive.

Segments are clipped, archived, reposted, embedded, monetized, and resurfaced indefinitely. Context erodes. Intent disappears. The original broadcast becomes one moment in a long chain of distribution.

Persistence did not create new liability rules. It exposed existing ones.

Civil law has always cared about what was said, what was copied, and what harm resulted. Digital circulation simply makes those questions easier to litigate and harder to escape.

The FCC did not lose authority. Exposure expanded.

Platforms Are Not a Shield

Modern confusion is compounded by platform immunity.

Under Section 230, platforms may be shielded from liability for hosting user-generated content. Creators are not.

A social media company may avoid responsibility for what it carries. The person who created the content does not.

This often fuels false confidence. Content spreads without consequence, and endurance is mistaken for approval. In reality, enforcement reflects complaint systems, resource limits, and selective attention, not legal validation.

The platform may be immune when it functions as a passive host. The creator never is.

Two Systems, One Risk

Broadcasters answer to two authorities: one regulating how they operate, and one judging the legal consequences of what they publish.

Online creators answer to one, and it is unforgiving.

Passing a regulatory test does not affect a civil one. Satisfying one system does not neutralize the other. Treating compliance as protection is how risk quietly accumulates.

The chapters that follow assume this separation.

From here forward, the analysis turns away from format and toward function: how courts evaluate purpose, transformation, amount, and market effect when copying occurs.

Regulation explains how media operates.

Liability explains how media harms.

Confusing the two is how professionals get blindsided.

Chapter Eight

FACTOR ONE: PURPOSE AND CHARACTER OF THE USE

Of all the fair use factors, purpose feels the most intuitive.

Creators know why they used a particular work and what they hoped that use would accomplish. They know whether it felt justified, responsible, or necessary in the moment. That sense of purpose often becomes the foundation of a creator's confidence.

It is also where fair use arguments most often begin to unravel.

Creators often equate purpose with intent. They assume commentary, criticism, journalism, or education automatically qualifies a use as fair.

It does not, at least not as a blanket rule. The law evaluates those purposes narrowly and in context, not as categorical exemptions.

This disconnect begins with where meaning is located. Creators tend to reason inwardly, focusing on intent, their motivation, justification, and professional identity. Courts reason outward. They reconstruct purpose from observable conduct, audience experience, and practical effect.

Courts do not decide cases by asking whether a creator felt justified, acted sincerely, or believed the use was fair. They look sideways, to evidence, structure, and consequence, and ask how the use functioned in the world. That is where purpose is found.

Purpose Is Not Intent

Purpose matters in fair use analysis, but not in the way creators often expect.

Courts do not treat purpose as a statement of belief. They treat it as a description of function. The question is not what the creator hoped to accomplish, but what the use actually did in relation to the original work and how the audience experienced that relationship.

A use can be critical and still be substitutive. A use can be journalistic and still be excessive. A use can involve real effort and still add nothing functionally new. Purpose supports fair use only when it changes the role the copied material plays.

Transformation Is Functional, Not Emotional

Transformation is the centerpiece of Factor One, and it is also the most misunderstood concept in modern media.

Creators often treat transformation as a feeling. If the use required work, judgment, or personality, it feels transformed. If it includes commentary or reaction, it feels different from the original.

That subjective sense may matter to the creator. It does not control the analysis.

Legal standards do not turn on effort, emotion, or sincerity. Courts evaluate transformation as an objective question: whether the copied material performs a different function than it did before.

This distinction matters most in "Play the Clip" formats, where reaction and commentary are layered onto copied material that still does the primary work for the audience.

If the clip supplies the value the audience came for, commentary does not transform it. If the clip anchors engagement, retains attention, or delivers the experience of the original, the use begins to look less like analysis and more like substitution.

Effort, reaction, and personality do not equal transformation.

Modern platforms reward all three. Algorithms favor familiarity, recognizability, and immediate payoff. That incentive structure explains why creators mistake engagement for transformation, and why courts do not.

Audience Experience Controls the Analysis

Creators often narrate purpose from their own perspective. Courts resolve it from the perspective of the audience.

If the audience no longer needs the original after consuming the secondary work, the fair use claim weakens. If the secondary use delivers the expressive value the audience seeks, purpose erodes.

This analysis operates on a sliding scale. The more a use is functionally necessary to resolve confusion, convey critical information, or prevent misunderstanding, and the less it can be replaced by description or summary, the more purpose carries weight. That justification narrows once necessity gives way to convenience.

This outward focus is not unique to copyright. Trademark law has long asked whether consumers are likely to be confused about source, sponsorship, or affiliation. Intent does not control that inquiry. Effect does.

Fair use analysis under Factor One operates in the same register. Courts are not concerned with how carefully a creator explains themselves. They are concerned with how the use is experienced in practice: whether it clarifies or replaces.

From the beginning, broadcast standards were justified by reference to the public, the listener, the viewer, the citizen. Modern courts use different language, but they ask a related question.

How did the audience experience the use?

That inquiry reflects an implied duty long familiar to talk media: the responsibility not to substitute consumption for understanding. Fair use did not invent that concern. It reframed it.

Journalism Is Relevant, Not Dispositive

Journalistic purpose can support fair use. It does not immunize it.

News reporting may justify copying when expression is necessary to convey information that cannot reasonably be communicated another way. Facts themselves are not protected. No one owns basic truth.

But reporting facts is not the same thing as reproducing expression. Courts distinguish between conveying information and delivering content. When a report relies on the expressive choices of another, the clip, the phrasing, the performance, the analysis shifts.

Modern media increasingly collapses distinctions between news, opinion, and entertainment. That convergence complicates fair use analysis, because purpose becomes harder to separate from engagement. When information delivery blends into performance, courts focus less on labels and more on function.

Newsworthiness explains why a topic matters. It does not explain how much expression may be taken or what role that expression plays.

Where Confidence Accumulates

Factor One is where creators feel safest because it aligns with professional identity. Commentary feels analytical. Journalism feels protected. Critique feels justified.

That confidence often persists even as other factors quietly turn against the use.

Purpose does not operate alone. It interacts with amount, selection, and market effect. When a use relies heavily on the most expressive portions of a work, purpose carries less weight. When a use supplies the value the audience seeks, purpose erodes further.

Creators rarely see that erosion as it happens. They feel purposeful right up until the analysis collapses.

What Factor One Can - and Cannot - Do

Factor One can support fair use. It rarely decides it.

Purpose can justify limited copying when expression is necessary to make a point that cannot be made otherwise. It cannot excuse convenience, completeness, or substitution. It cannot rescue a use that delivers the original's value under the banner of commentary.

Understanding that limitation does not make creators timid. It makes them accurate.

The next chapters examine where purpose most often overreaches: when amount expands, when selection sharpens, and when market impact becomes unavoidable. Purpose may open the door to fair use analysis.

It does not carry the argument through it.

Chapter Nine

FACTOR TWO: NATURE OF THE ORIGINAL WORK

Factor Two is often treated as the quiet factor. The one courts mention briefly. The one creators skip mentally. The one that rarely appears to decide anything on its own.

That perception is understandable but incomplete.

Factor Two is rarely the opening move and almost never the sole reason a case is won or lost. But when the analysis tightens, when purpose is plausible, amount is restrained, and market effect is contested, this is the factor that can decide the outcome.

It is the late-stage variable. The one that matters most when everything else is close.

Why Factor Two Exists

Copyright does not protect all works equally.

That statement can sound like a value judgment. It is not. It is structural.

Some works sit closer to raw information. Others are built from creative judgment: choices about phrasing, sequencing, emphasis, performance, or presentation. The closer a work is to original expression, the less tolerance courts have for unlicensed copying.

Factor Two exists to recognize that difference.

It does not ask whether a work is important, influential, or widely circulated. It asks what kind of work it is and how much creative authorship it embodies. That inquiry shapes the analysis that follows.

"Factual" Is Not a Safe Category

Creators often assume factual works occupy safer ground. News reports, interviews, speeches, and informational segments are frequently treated as raw material rather than authored expression.

Courts do not see them that way.

Facts themselves are not protected. Expression is. Expression exists even when a work communicates information. Choices about what to include, what to omit, how to phrase, how to sequence, and how to emphasize all reflect creative judgment.

A work can be factual in purpose and expressive in execution at the same time.

This is why labeling material as "news" or "informational" does not resolve Factor Two. Courts look past the label and examine how much authorship is present in the original work.

Publication Does Not Equal Permission

Another common assumption is that publication changes the analysis. Once a work is broadcast, posted, or widely shared, creators often treat it as fair game.

Publication matters. It does not authorize copying.

Courts distinguish between availability and ownership. A published work may be easier to reference, quote, or discuss, but its expressive elements remain protected. Factor Two does not reward wide circulation. In some cases it does the opposite, recognizing that a work's expressive value may be heightened by its reach.

Public access is not the public domain.

Spontaneity Is Still Expression

This distinction is especially important in talk and broadcast media.

Live interviews, unscripted commentary, and spontaneous exchanges are often treated as raw facts captured in real time. Creators sometimes assume that because something was not scripted or polished, it is less protected.

Courts reject that assumption.

Spontaneous speech still reflects authorship. Tone, phrasing, cadence, emphasis, and delivery all contribute to creative expression. An off-the-cuff remark can be as expressive as a prepared statement. A live exchange can carry more creative value than a written one.

Factor Two does not discount expression simply because it happened quickly.

How Factor Two Narrows the Margin

Factor Two rarely ends the analysis. Instead, it defines the size of the field.

It does not function as a separate test. It functions as a variable that changes how much leverage the other factors have.

When a source work reflects substantial creative judgment, courts expect greater restraint in every other factor. Purpose must be tighter. Amount must be smaller. Market impact must be harder to show.

When a work sits closer to raw information, the field widens slightly.

It never disappears.

This is why some uses fail even when purpose is legitimate and copying feels modest. The original work simply left less room to maneuver.

What Factor Two Is and Is Not

Factor Two does not say that factual works are free, that published works are safe, or that live speech is unprotected.

It says something narrower and more predictive.

Some works leave less room to borrow than creators expect.

The next chapter turns to where that narrowing becomes unavoidable once market effect enters the analysis. At that point, even careful discipline may not overcome the limits Factor Two quietly imposed.

Factor Two rarely decides cases.

It explains why they were harder than they appeared.

Chapter Ten

FACTOR THREE: AMOUNT AND SUBSTANTIALITY OF THE PORTION USED

If purpose is where confidence begins, amount is where it most often collapses.

Creators tend to think of amount as a math problem. Seconds. Words. Percentages. Shorter feels safer. Partial feels restrained. A clip feels different from a copy.

Courts do not evaluate amount that way.

Factor Three is not about how long something runs. It is about how much expressive value was taken and whether what was taken was necessary to serve the claimed purpose.

That distinction is why so many fair use arguments fail even when intent is strong and commentary is real.

The Quantity Myth

The most common misunderstanding of fair use is the belief that small uses are presumptively safe.

They are not.

Courts have rejected percentage-based reasoning for decades. There is no safe fraction. There is no minimum that guarantees protection. A short excerpt can be infringing if it captures the essence of the work. A longer excerpt can sometimes survive if it is functionally justified.

Length is not the metric. Function is.

Creators fixate on duration because it is measurable, while courts focus on substantiality because it is meaningful.

Amount Is Qualitative, Not Arithmetic

Factor Three asks two related questions:

How much of the original work was taken?

How important was what was taken?

The second question often matters more.

Taking the "heart" of a work, the most memorable, expressive, or valuable portion, can outweigh restraint elsewhere. A few seconds of a signature moment may carry more weight than minutes of background material.

This is why amount cannot be evaluated in isolation. What matters is not just how much was used, but what role that portion plays in the original work and in the secondary use.

When the excerpt delivers the value the audience came for, amount becomes substantial regardless of duration.

Selection Is Evidence

Creators often think of clips as neutral. Courts do not.

Selection is an editorial act. Choosing which portion to use reveals judgment, priority, and intent. Courts infer meaning from that choice.

Using the most compelling portion of a work suggests that the expressive core mattered. Using the climactic moment suggests substitution. Using the quote everyone remembers suggests that recognition, not explanation, drove the decision.

This is why highlights are legally dangerous. They concentrate value. They compress experience. They give audiences what they want most with the least friction.

Restraint is not about choosing less. It is about choosing only what is necessary, even when that choice makes the secondary work less engaging.

Necessity Is the Only Durable Justification

Amount carries weight only when necessity is doing the work.

Courts ask whether the amount taken was reasonably required to achieve the stated purpose. Could the point have been made with less? Could it have been described instead of shown? Could context have been conveyed without reproducing expression?

The more a use relies on convenience, efficiency, or audience expectation, the weaker the justification becomes. The more it relies on necessity, to prevent confusion, to convey precise meaning, or to explain something that cannot reasonably be paraphrased, the more amount is tolerated.

This is not a moral judgment. It is a functional one.

Modern Formats Intensify the Risk

Contemporary media formats magnify Factor Three problems by design.

Clips, reels, compilations, and "best of" segments are built around extraction. They privilege recognition over explanation and completeness over context. They reward delivering the most expressive parts of a work quickly and efficiently.

That does not make them unlawful. It makes them fragile.

In these formats, amount and selection often work together to recreate the original experience in compressed form. When that happens, restraint disappears even when the creator adds original commentary intended to contextualize or justify the use.

The legal analysis does not change because the medium is new. The exposure increases because the use delivers more value with less material.

The deeper implications of platform incentives and distribution mechanics are addressed later in this guide. Here, the takeaway is simpler: modern formats make it easier to take too much without realizing it.

Amount Escalates Even Strong Uses

Factor Three often defeats fair use claims that survive Factor One.

Even when purpose is legitimate.

Even when commentary is real.

Even when intent is sincere.

Using more than necessary, or selecting the most expressive material, can tip the analysis against the creator. Amount does not operate independently. It amplifies the weaknesses of the other factors.

Creators rarely experience this escalation in real time. Amount feels modest right up until it is decisive.

What Factor Three Demands

Factor Three does not demand minimalism for its own sake.

It demands discipline.

Using only what is required.

Avoiding the most expressive moments when they are not essential.

Accepting that explanation may be less engaging than reproduction.

Those choices are rarely intuitive. They are rarely rewarded by platforms. But they are central to how courts evaluate amount and substantiality.

The next chapter examines where these tensions finally resolve: when the law asks whether the use displaced the original in the marketplace.

Chapter Eleven

FACTOR FOUR: EFFECT ON THE POTENTIAL MARKET

Factor Four is where fair use arguments most often collapse.

Not because courts distrust commentary, criticism, or journalism, but because this factor forces the analysis outward, away from intention, effort, and justification, and toward consequences.

Factor Four asks a question that is difficult to avoid:

What did this use do to the market for the original work?

That question explains why this factor so often anchors the analysis.

Why Market Effect Carries Disproportionate Weight

Copyright is not a moral system. It is an economic one.

Factor Four aligns most directly with that reality. It allows courts to assess whether a use interferes with the copyright owner's ability to exploit the work, now or in the future, regardless of how the use was framed.

This is not about punishing creators. It is about preserving the structure that allows creative markets to function.

Courts rely on this factor because it focuses on outcomes rather than explanations.

What "Market" Actually Means

Creators often interpret "market" too narrowly. They look for lost sales, declining revenue, or direct competition.

Courts do not.

Market effect includes harm to the following:

- existing markets
- potential markets
- derivative markets
- customary or reasonably foreseeable licensing markets

The inquiry is not whether the original creator lost money. It is whether the use interfered with a market the copyright owner is entitled to control.

That control includes markets the owner has not yet entered but reasonably could.

Examples of Potential Markets

Potential markets are not speculative. They are ordinary extensions of creative exploitation.

Courts routinely recognize markets such as:

- licensing excerpts for broadcast or online use
- paid speaking engagements or appearances built around the work
- monetized YouTube or podcast channels operated by the creator
- clip licensing for documentaries, retrospectives, or commentary
- derivative educational, archival, or promotional uses
- controlled reposting or syndication of the work itself

A creator does not need to be actively exploiting each of these markets. The question is whether allowing unlicensed use would reasonably impair the ability to do so.

The law protects that option value.

Reasonable Likelihood Is Enough

Creators often assume market harm must be large, provable, or dramatic.

It does not.

Courts require a reasonable likelihood of market harm, not certainty. And the harm does not need to be enormous. It needs to be economically meaningful in context.

A use that undercuts a licensing market, weakens demand for authorized versions, or normalizes unpaid substitution can satisfy Factor Four even if the dollar amounts are modest.

Copyright does not require owners to tolerate small losses simply because they are small.

Substitution Is the Core Concern

At the heart of Factor Four is substitution.

If a secondary use satisfies audience demand for the original, courts presume harm. That presumption does not depend on identical format or identical audience. It turns on function.

A use can substitute by:

- delivering the most expressive or memorable portion of the work
- providing sufficient access that audiences no longer seek the original
- repeatedly supplying value the original would otherwise provide

Substitution can be cumulative. Individual uses may appear trivial. Patterns are not. Courts evaluate that accumulation.

The Fallacy of Harmlessness

Creators frequently argue that their use caused no harm because:

- it promoted the original
- it reached a larger or different audience
- it increased visibility or awareness
- it was done in good faith

Courts are unmoved.

Promotion does not negate substitution. Reaching a new audience does not eliminate market interference. And good intentions do not neutralize economic effect.

These arguments share the same flaw. They rely on intent rather than outcome.

Factor Four removes intent from the equation.

Who Decides on Market Strategy

Creators sometimes argue that:

- the copyright owner would not have licensed this use
- the owner lost nothing by allowing it
- the use benefits everyone

Courts respond with a simpler principle.

Copyright owners, not users, decide how their works are monetized.

That includes deciding:

- whether a market exists
- whether a license is offered
- whether exposure is desirable
- whether exclusivity has value

Fair use does not transfer that decision-making authority.

Cumulative Effect and Scale

Factor Four is uniquely sensitive to scale.

Courts consider not just what happened here, but what would happen if similar uses became common. Would the practice undermine licensing norms? Would it erode incentives to create or distribute the work? Would it displace markets systematically?

This scaling matters even when the individual use feels modest.

Creators assess risk case by case. Courts assess impact system-wide.

How Factor Four Interacts with the Others

Factor Four often resolves cases where the other factors point in different directions.

A legitimate purpose under Factor One does not excuse market substitution.

Restraint under Factor Three does not eliminate displacement.

Expressive originals under Factor Two often make markets more fragile, not less.

When the analysis tightens, this factor often decides the case.

What Factor Four Ultimately Demands

Factor Four does not require creators to eliminate risk. It requires them to recognize where risk concentrates.

Uses that explain rather than reproduce are safer. Uses that rely on necessity rather than convenience are safer. Uses that avoid satisfying audience demand for the original are safer.

None of these are guarantees.

Factor Four is where fair use arguments shift from justification to consequence.

Creators often reach that realization too late.

Courts do not.

Chapter Twelve

HOW THE FACTORS ACTUALLY WORK TOGETHER

By this point, the factors should feel familiar. Purpose. Nature. Amount. Market effect. What may be less obvious is that they were never meant to operate separately. Each has its own vocabulary, its own pressure points, and its own ways of surprising creators who believed they were on solid ground.

What matters now is how they operate together.

Fair use is not additive. It is not a scorecard. And it is not a system where enough good intentions can cancel out a bad result.

Courts do not tally factors. They evaluate how they interact.

Why the Factors Are Not Independent

The four factors are often presented as separate questions. That presentation is convenient. It is also misleading.

In practice, the factors function as a system. Each one shapes how the others are understood. Strength in one factor can raise expectations in the others. Weakness in another can amplify risk across the analysis.

This is why fair use outcomes can feel unpredictable to creators while remaining internally consistent in judicial reasoning. The factors do not operate in isolation. They operate in relation to one another.

The Chain, Not the Checklist

Courts often reason through the factors as a chain of dependency.

Purpose frames the story.

Nature defines the margin.

Amount tests discipline.

Market effect anchors the outcome.

This is not an order of importance. It reflects how the factors interact in judicial practice.

A legitimate purpose under Factor One does not excuse unnecessary copying under Factor Three. A restrained excerpt under Factor Three does not neutralize substitution under Factor Four. And expressive originals under Factor Two narrow tolerance everywhere else.

Once that chain breaks, the analysis rarely recovers.

Why Isolated Strength Fails

Creators often approach fair use defensively, pointing to individual strengths as if they were shields.

The purpose was commentary.

The amount was short.

The use felt transformative.

Courts respond by asking harder questions.

Commentary that did what?

Short compared to what?

Transformative for whom?

When those answers are evaluated together, confidence built on a single factor erodes quickly.

Fair use arguments fail most often not because every factor cuts against the creator, but because one factor collapses under the weight of the others.

The Role of Necessity Across the Analysis

Necessity is the constraint that stabilizes the analysis.

Necessity disciplines purpose by tying justification to function rather than identity.

Necessity constrains amount by requiring restraint beyond convenience.

Necessity limits market harm by preventing substitution rather than explaining it away.

When necessity is present, the factors reinforce one another. When it is absent, they unravel quickly.

This is why courts repeatedly return to what could have been done differently, not what the creator hoped to achieve.

Why Fair Use Feels Inconsistent

Creators often describe fair use as unpredictable. That perception usually comes from focusing on outcomes rather than structure.

From the outside, two uses can look similar. From the court's perspective, small differences in purpose, selection, or effect can cascade through the analysis. A slight increase in amount can trigger market harm analysis. A more expressive source work can narrow tolerance. A stronger market can raise expectations of restraint.

The system is not random. It is sensitive.

What the System Is Actually Protecting

Fair use exists to preserve breathing room without collapsing markets. It allows criticism without authorizing substitution. It permits commentary without converting copyrighted works into raw material.

The factors reflect that balance. They are not designed to reward effort or sincerity. They are designed to prevent uses that undermine the structure copyright depends on to function.

Once that purpose is understood, the outcomes make more sense even when they are uncomfortable.

Where This Leaves the Creator

Fair use does not ask whether a creator meant well. It asks whether the use functioned in a way the system can tolerate.

That question is not answered by confidence, habit, or platform norms. It is answered by how the factors interact under scrutiny.

Understanding that interaction does not make fair use safe. It makes the system legible.

That is the point of this guide.

INTERLUDE

FROM MURROW TO THE TIMELINE: WHY SELECTION MATTERS

Long before digital platforms, broadcast journalists understood that clip selection was an editorial act, even if they never paused to explain it to the audience. Often, the editorial judgment lay in selecting a particular instance or actuality.

In the era of Walter Cronkite and Edward R. Murrow, interviews were rarely aired in full. Time constraints alone made that impossible. Instead, producers and editors listened, debated, and chose specific excerpts that captured what they believed mattered most. The audience was not meant to hear everything. They were meant to hear what the newsroom judged essential.

Cronkite spoke often about the responsibility of compression, the obligation to distill complex events without distorting them. While he rarely narrated the mechanics of clip selection on air, he described the anchor's role as one of judgment rather than neutral transmission. The task was not to reproduce events verbatim, but to present their most meaningful elements with accuracy and restraint.

Murrow took the idea even further. In his 1958 RTNDA speech, "Wires and Lights in a Box," he warned broadcasters that television's power lay not in its ability to show everything, but in the human choices that shaped what viewers saw. Images and sounds, he argued, required context. Without it, broadcasting risked becoming spectacle instead of journalism.

By the late 1960s, political coverage had given this practice a name: the "sound bite." The term itself assumes selection. A sound bite is not accidental. It is a fragment chosen for its impact, extracted from a longer whole, and placed deliberately within a larger narrative.

Network training manuals from the period reflect the same understanding. Editors were taught to cut interviews for clarity, relevance, and fairness, not merely to shorten them. Selection was treated as an act of authorship, carrying responsibility for how meaning would be received.

In the analog era, this discipline was unavoidable. Tape was scarce. Airtime was finite. Every cut destroyed something else. Selection carried weight because it had to.

Today, abundance has replaced scarcity, but the legal logic has not changed. Choosing a clip is still an expressive act. Fair use begins with that choice.

What has changed since Cronkite and Murrow is not the act of selection, but the legal exposure attached to it. "Play the Clip" has survived from analog control rooms into digital feeds. The law has followed it and now asks creators to justify not just what they chose, but why.

Chapter Thirteen

HOW WORKFLOW QUIETLY CREATES RISK

If Chapter 12 explained how the factors interact, this chapter explains where that analysis most often breaks down in practice. Infringement in modern media is rarely intentional.

Creators understand the rules. They know the vocabulary. They can explain the factors. Yet infringement still occurs, not because the law is unclear, but because analysis gives way to routine.

Risk does not usually enter through bad intent. It enters when workflow replaces judgment.

When Analysis Becomes Habit

Fair use analysis requires a pause. Workflow rewards speed. Virality collapses that pause entirely.

As creators gain experience, decisions that once required thought become instinctive. Clips are selected quickly. Segments are reused without reconsideration. Formats repeat. The friction that once forced evaluation disappears.

That efficiency feels like progress. Legally, it reads as exposure.

Courts do not evaluate how a decision felt at the time it was made. They evaluate what was used, how it was used, and what effect it had. Experience does not excuse the absence of analysis.

Familiar Formats Create False Confidence

Certain formats feel safe because they are familiar.

Reaction videos. Clip commentary. Segment reposting. Highlight reels. Short excerpts embedded inside critique. Audio pulled from longer conversations and reused across platforms.

These formats are not inherently unlawful, but familiarity dulls scrutiny.

Creators begin to substitute format for analysis. If the structure matches a familiar template, reaction, commentary, or critique, the legal inquiry is treated as already resolved. The work becomes formulaic, optimized for repetition and distribution rather than reassessed for its function.

Courts do not evaluate format. They evaluate function.

The Confidence Trap

As workflows mature, confidence increases.

Decisions are made faster. Judgment becomes intuitive. The same types of content are handled the same way, over and over, without renewed scrutiny. What once felt like a legal choice becomes a production step.

Internal validation is meaningless if the finished product fails under scrutiny. Confidence does not travel with the work into court.

Where Risk Accumulates

Risk accumulates at the seams, where individual decisions are stitched together into a finished product that no longer fits its original justification.

When clips are reused across platforms without reassessing audience or market effect.

When excerpts are shortened but made more expressive.

When commentary is added once and assumed to justify later reuse.

As clips are cropped, condensed, or repurposed, the use changes, but the original justification is carried forward without reconsideration. What began as one use becomes another.

Courts look at the whole picture, informed by decades of adjudicated uses, while creators often see only their final step in isolation.

Normalization Is Not Neutral

Practices that feel normal stop being questioned.

When a workflow becomes standard, the legal analysis that once accompanied it fades into the background. Decisions are justified by habit rather than necessity.

Normalization does not make a practice lawful. It makes it invisible.

Courts do not care whether a practice is widespread. They care whether it is justified.

What Courts Actually See

Courts do not see the process behind a decision. They see only what appears on the record, the material used, the way it was presented, and the effect it had.

They do not care how the decision was made. If the use is not justified on its face, the explanation behind it carries little weight.

Why This Chapter Matters

Fair use does not fail at the level of principle. It fails at the level of practice, when judgment is replaced by repetition and analysis is assumed rather than performed.

The chapters that follow examine how these failures surface in specific contexts, not to shame formats but to make visible what habit tends to hide.

Chapter Fourteen

WHEN RECONSTRUCTION BECOMES SUBSTITUTION

Creators do not set out to replace someone else's work. Fair use analysis exists because substitution rarely announces itself as replacement.

What they do instead is contribute, remix, explain, react, curate, stitch, and reassemble material in ways that feel additive rather than competitive. The intent is rarely to stand in for the original. The problem is that intent does not determine effect.

Substitution does not begin with copying too much. It begins with rebuilding too well.

Reconstruction Is the Hidden Mechanism

Substitution rarely happens all at once. It happens through reconstruction.

A clip here. A highlight there. A pause for commentary. Another excerpt to clarify context. Another to complete the thought. Over time, the audience no longer needs to seek out the original work to understand it, experience it, or extract its value.

What looks like commentary at the clip level can become reconstruction at the format level.

Courts describe the result as substitution. Creators experience it as completeness.

Why Replacement Rarely Feels Like Replacement

Replacement sounds intentional. Substitution usually is not.

Creators tend to evaluate their use from the inside out. They focus on effort, insight, and presentation. They ask whether they added value, offered perspective, or improved understanding. Those questions feel decisive. They are not.

From the audience's perspective, the question is simpler: is there anything left to go get?

When a use delivers the most important moments, the emotional core, or the informational substance of the original, the audience's need changes. At that point, the use is no longer adjacent. It begins to function as a stand-in.

That is replacement in practice. Courts call it substitution.

Aggregation Changes the Analysis

Individual excerpts often appear defensible in isolation. Aggregation changes that.

A single clip may not substitute. A sequence of clips might. A short excerpt may be justified. A curated progression of excerpts can recreate the experience the original provided.

Reconstruction does not require copying everything. It requires copying what matters.

When the use captures the decisive moments, the essential narrative, or the most valuable portions of a work, it begins to serve the same function as the original. That is where fair use arguments start to collapse.

Added Value Does Not Prevent Substitution

Creators frequently argue that their use is fair because they added something.

They clarified meaning. Improved accessibility. Streamlined understanding. Injected personality. Made the content more efficient.

Those arguments misunderstand the inquiry.

Improvement does not negate substitution. Curation does not negate substitution. Accessibility does not negate substitution.

A use can add value and still compete. In some cases, added value accelerates substitution by making the original unnecessary.

Audience Perspective Is Decisive

Courts evaluate substitution from the audience's point of view, not the creator's.

The question is not whether commentary was added. The question is whether the use absorbed the role the original work played in the marketplace.

If the audience can receive the substance of the original without seeking it out, substitution has occurred, even if the creator believes the use was contextual rather than competitive.

Partial Substitution Is Enough

Partial substitution often operates through metonymy, where a part comes to stand in for the whole. A single scene represents an entire film. A key exchange captures the substance of a longer interview. A decisive moment carries the meaning of an extended work.

When a use extracts and presents those representative elements, the audience may feel they have already received what matters. At that point, the part is no longer incidental. It is functioning as the whole.

Replacing the most valuable portion of a work can be enough. Replacing the emotional payoff can be enough. Replacing the informational function can be enough.

Fair use fails most often when creators assume that because they did not copy everything, they did not replace anything.

Where Liability Enters

Not every use substitutes. But when a use absorbs the core function of the original, it crosses a boundary.

At that point, the use is no longer part of a larger discussion. It is no longer supporting commentary. It is performing the work the original once did.

That is where liability attaches.

The chapters that follow examine how monetization, amplification, and repetition accelerate this process and why substitution becomes harder to avoid as distribution expands.

Chapter Fifteen

MONETIZATION, AMPLIFICATION, AND THE GRAVITY OF MARKETS

Monetization does not convert a defensible use into infringement.

But once money and scope enter the picture, weaknesses in a fair use argument become harder to ignore.

What once felt incidental begins to look purposeful. What once felt harmless begins to look competitive.

The law does not change. The stakes do.

Why Money Sharpens Scrutiny

Creators often think about monetization in binary terms. Either they sold the clip, or they did not. Either the audience paid, or it was free.

Courts do not frame the question that way.

The inquiry is whether the use contributed to commercial gain, directly or indirectly, by attracting attention, building audience, or strengthening a revenue stream tied to the creator.

That assessment is economic, not moral.

Commercial Benefit Without Selling the Work

A use can generate commercial benefits without charging for access.

Advertising revenue. Sponsorships. Subscriptions. Brand growth. Audience loyalty leading to future monetization.

None of these require selling the copied work itself. They require only that the work help generate value for the user.

Fair use analysis follows value, not labels.

Self-Use Is Not Third-Party Use

There is a critical distinction creators often blur.

Using clips from your own show to promote your work is fundamentally different from using someone else's work to promote yourself.

When a creator excerpts their own material, they are marketing the same work, the same audience relationship, and the same underlying rights. No competing market is displaced. No third-party value is absorbed.

Using someone else's work, even with attribution, even with commentary, even if the original creator receives platform monetization credit, is different. The attention flows to the user. The audience relationship is captured by the user. The value accrues to the user's channel, brand, or business.

Giving credit does not give back time.

Time Is Finite

Courts do not assume a fixed amount of money in the world. They do assume finite markets.

Time, attention, and audience focus are limited resources.

In a crowded media environment, every minute matters. Every minute spent consuming a reconstructed or substituted version of a work is a minute not spent engaging with the original.

That reality does not require proving that someone lost a job or missed a paycheck. It requires recognizing that demand operates within limits.

Copyright law accounts for that.

Opportunity Cost Cannot Be Ignored

Market harm is not limited to lost sales.

Opportunity cost is real.

Lost licensing opportunities.

Weakened negotiating leverage.

Reduced incentive to distribute or license.

Erosion of derivative or emerging markets.

These harms are structural and often leave no paper trail. Courts do not require a canceled contract to recognize them.

A use that absorbs attention, satisfies demand, or redirects audience behavior can impose opportunity costs even when the market continues to grow.

Amplification Changes Function

Scale alters how a use operates.

A use that might be tolerable once can become problematic when repeated, amplified, or normalized. Distribution reshapes audience habits. What begins as reference can become the default. What begins as commentary can become the primary source.

Amplification does not create substitution on its own. It accelerates it.

The Free Content Fallacy

Creators often argue that their use is harmless because the content is free.

Free does not mean neutral.

A free substitute can still divert demand. A free reconstruction can still satisfy audience needs. A free alternative can still erode markets.

Price is not the measure. Function is.

Repetition and Normalization

Repeated uses change behavior.

Audiences learn where to go first. Expectations form. The original sources fade into the background.

Over time, monetized reuse can reshape a market even if no single use seems decisive. Courts account for that cumulative effect.

What Courts Ultimately Evaluate

Courts do not assume that only one creator can succeed. But they recognize that markets are bounded enough to be displaced.

They ask whether a use meaningfully interferes with the markets copyright law is meant to protect, including present, derivative, and reasonably foreseeable ones.

That question becomes sharper when monetization and scope are involved because the economic consequences are clearer.

Why This Chapter Matters

This chapter is not about condemning creators for earning money.

In a time-scarce marketplace, using someone else's work to build attention, revenue, or brand equity has structural consequences.

The chapters that follow examine how platform structures and incentives intensify these pressures and why restraint becomes harder, not easier, as scope expands.

Chapter Sixteen

PLATFORMS, INCENTIVES, AND THE ILLUSION OF NEUTRALITY

Creators often think of platforms as neutral containers. Places where content lives. Tools that distribute what users choose to create.

The assumption is that they differ only in flavor, like ice cream variations built on the same underlying mixture. But platforms are not flavor variations. They are engineered systems with distinct incentives built into their design.

Courts do not see them that way.

Not because platforms are defendants in most copyright cases. They usually are not. But because platforms shape how content is created, repeated, amplified, and monetized. Those structural conditions matter even when the platform itself is not on trial.

This chapter is about that gap.

What the System Actually Amplifies

It is common to say that platforms amplify "what works."

That phrasing hides something important.

Platforms do not amplify content because it is lawful. They amplify content because it performs. Performance is defined internally through metrics designed to maximize engagement, retention, growth, and monetization.

What "works" is not determined by legal compliance, public value, or creative restraint. It is determined by whether users stay longer, click more, share faster, and return more often.

That definition is not accidental. It reflects the incentives platforms ultimately answer to.

Incentives Flow Upward, Risk Flows Downward

Platforms are accountable to shareholders. That is not a criticism. It is a fact of corporate structure.

Creators, by contrast, bear the legal risk of what they publish.

This creates a quiet asymmetry. A platform can discourage infringement in its terms while structurally rewarding the behaviors that lead to it. Reuse. Familiarity. Emotional completeness. Recognizable clips that perform well with minimal explanation.

The system does not need users to break the law. It only needs them to take risks the platform does not carry.

The Myth of Alignment

There is a widespread assumption that platforms do not want users to violate the law.

That assumption is only partly true.

Platforms do not want liability. Risk that falls elsewhere does not affect them in the same way. A use that increases engagement but shifts legal exposure onto the creator does not register as a problem in the same way.

Courts are not confused by this distinction. Platform permission is not legal permission. Automated distribution is not authorization.

Why Neutral Tools Produce Non-Neutral Outcomes

Platforms may be neutral in design intent. They are not neutral in effect.

Algorithms amplify patterns. Patterns normalize behavior. Normalized behavior becomes workflow.

Over time, creators learn what is rewarded and adapt accordingly. Not because they are reckless, but because speed, consistency, and familiarity are built into the system.

That adaptation is understandable.

It is also legally irrelevant.

Process Disappears. Output Remains

Creators experience platforms from the inside as workflows, dashboards, analytics, and feedback loops.

Courts encounter only the finished product.

They do not see the edits that were rejected.

They do not see the pauses that were skipped.

They do not see the pressure to post again tomorrow.

They see what was published, how often, how widely, and how it functioned in the marketplace.

The process disappears. The finished work is all that remains.

Why This Matters for Fair Use

Fair use analysis does not ask whether a platform encouraged a use. It asks what the use did.

Did it repeat?

Did it substitute?

Did it satisfy audience demand?

Did it interfere with markets?

Those questions do not change because the system made the decision easier, faster, or more profitable.

The Diagnostic Takeaway

Platforms do not force infringement. But their incentive structures reward behaviors that can lead toward it.

They reward speed over pause.

Recognition over restraint.

Performance over proportionality.

Understanding that dynamic does not excuse creators. It explains why risk clusters where it does.

The chapters that follow address what happens next, when immunity, automation, and enforcement asymmetry enter the picture, and why the law assigns responsibility where it does regardless of how the system feels from the inside.

Chapter Seventeen

PLATFORM IMMUNITY AND CREATOR LIABILITY ARE DIFFERENT THINGS

Every minute, hundreds of hours of video are uploaded to YouTube. Thousands of podcast episodes are published. Millions of posts, clips, and excerpts move through platforms without human review.

At that rate, YouTube alone uploads more video in roughly thirty-two hours than a person could watch in a lifetime.

That scale is not incidental. It is the reason platform immunity exists in the first place.

Creators encounter that scale from the inside. Courts evaluate it from the outside. The difference matters.

How the Mistake Forms

Creators often observe three things. The platform hosts the content. The platform distributes it. The platform monetizes it.

From there, a conclusion forms. If the platform allowed it, the platform must have approved it. If the platform profited, it is not unreasonable to assume the platform absorbed the risk. And if the platform is protected, surely the creator should be too.

The law assigns responsibility differently.

What This Chapter Is - and Is Not

The statutory frameworks governing platform immunity, including the DMCA safe harbor system and Section 230, are complex and frequently misunderstood. They are addressed in detail elsewhere. This chapter does not attempt to resolve those debates.

Its purpose is narrower.

This chapter explains why platform immunity and creator liability coexist without contradiction, and why confusing the two produces false confidence that fails when a dispute actually arises.

Procedural Insulation Is Not Permission

Platform immunity provides procedural insulation. It allows platforms to operate automated hosting and distribution processes at volume without evaluating each piece of content before it appears.

That protection exists because the volume of content makes individualized review unworkable.

Creator liability addresses something else entirely: use.

What was copied.

How it was presented.

What role it played.

What effect it had.

Passing content through insulated processes does not convert it into lawful use. It explains only how it moved through the system.

Why Silence Feels Like Validation

Creators often read platform silence as approval.

Content stays live. It gets recommended. It generates comments. It earns revenue.

In environments where users are quick to react, the absence of backlash feels like confirmation. If something were truly wrong, surely someone would say so.

But outrage is not legal judgment.

Silence is not clearance.

Engagement is not approval.

Platforms read performance signals. They do not evaluate legality.

Scale Explains Continued Exposure

Platforms operate at volumes that make individualized legal judgment impossible. Enforcement is selective, delayed, automated, and often complaint driven.

Courts understand this.

What they do not do is infer legality from persistence.

A work's continued availability explains only that it has not yet triggered sufficient attention to prompt enforcement.

Scale explains continued exposure. It does not confer legal status.

Where Responsibility Actually Lands

Platforms manage risk through process. Creators bear risk through publication.

This can feel imbalanced. Platforms profit. Creators carry exposure.

But copyright law does not exist to measure fairness between parties. It assigns responsibility for acts of use, even when those acts occur inside efficient, automated distribution pipelines.

The Line That Matters

Platform immunity explains why content remains available.

It does not determine who is responsible for its use.

Once that distinction is understood, the analysis becomes clearer and far less forgiving.

The chapters that follow examine how automation, AI, and enforcement asymmetry intensify this divide, and why responsibility remains anchored to output even when the process feels invisible.

Chapter Eighteen

REPETITION IS THE RISK

Fair use does not usually fail all at once. It erodes through repetition, over time.

That erosion is rarely noticed by the creator while it is happening. Each individual decision feels small. Each use feels familiar. Each justification feels the same as the last one. But courts do not evaluate fair use as a series of isolated moments. They evaluate bodies of work.

That difference explains why creators are often surprised when a dispute arises. The problem was never a single clip. It was the pattern that formed quietly around it.

Courts Do Not Weigh Feelings

Creators tend to explain their work in terms of intention and experience. What they meant to do. Why the use felt justified. How the audience responded. Whether the commentary was sincere or valuable.

Courts give those explanations little weight.

They examine what is visible in the finished product. What was used. How often. How prominently. How it was framed. How consistently the same method appears across episodes, posts, or releases.

Warm explanations do not survive contact with the record. Only concrete facts do.

Accumulation Changes the Question

Most fair use problems do not begin as problems. They begin as habits.

A clip here. An image there. A brief excerpt to set context or illustrate a point. Each use may be defensible on its own. But repetition changes how those uses are perceived.

Over time, what looked like commentary begins to look like reliance. What looked like reference begins to look like structure. The analysis shifts without the creator ever noticing it has shifted.

Courts notice immediately.

Fair use does not fail loudly. It wears down gradually as the same choice is made again and again.

Growth Rewards the Wrong Things

Modern media rewards repetition. Platforms reward formats that perform. Audiences reward familiarity. Algorithms reward predictability.

Consider a common trajectory.

A show begins with original commentary. Occasionally, a clip is used to anchor discussion. Audience response is strong. Engagement increases. Over time, the clips that perform best become the backbone of the format.

Episodes are structured around them. The commentary adjusts to serve the clip rather than the other way around.

Growth improves. Legal defensibility does not.

Nothing about this evolution feels reckless from the inside. It feels professional. Responsive. data-driven. But fair use does not care whether a format performs well. It cares whether the use of third party material has become functionally necessary.

Growth rewards reliance. Fair use punishes reliance.

Professionalism Sharpens Exposure

As formats mature, production quality improves. Branding becomes consistent. Monetization stabilizes. The work looks deliberate.

That professionalism does not help in a fair use analysis. It hurts.

Consistency signals method. Polish signals intention. Sustainability signals participation in a market. Courts do not infer malice from professionalism, but they do infer knowledge. A creator who appears to know what they are doing is assumed to understand the rules governing reuse.

This is not a moral judgment. It is an evidentiary one.

When Use Becomes the Product

The most dangerous shift is also the quietest.

At a certain point, third party material stops supporting the content and starts carrying it. The original work becomes the hook, the draw, and the reason the audience shows up. Remove the clips and the format collapses.

This is not a DJ playing the hits. It is not incidental reference. It is a product built on other people's work.

Creators rarely experience this moment consciously. Courts encounter it fully formed.

The Diagnostic Takeaway

Fair use failures are not caused by bad actors or careless intent. They are caused by systems that reward speed, repetition, optimization, and growth.

Fair use doctrine rewards none of those things.

It asks whether the use added something meaningfully new, whether it relied on protected expression only as necessary, and whether it avoided substituting for the original in the marketplace.

That erosion is what this chapter makes visible.

Chapter Nineteen

FAIR USE IS A RISK DECISION, NOT A RULE

Fair use is judged on what the work does, not on what the creator hoped it would do.

The moment fair use enters the conversation, copying has already occurred. That is not an accusation. It is the legal posture. Fair use is not the absence of copying. It is a justification offered after copying has been established.

At that stage, there is no morally superior position. There is only exposure and explanation.

Creators often resist this framing because it feels backward. They did not set out to steal. They acted with purpose. They added commentary. They believed they were contributing something new.

None of that prevents infringement from existing.

Trying Is Not a Defense

Creators frequently treat effort as mitigation. If they worked hard, thought carefully, or acted sincerely, the use feels defensible. It feels earned.

Courts do not evaluate effort. They evaluate outcome.

A careful infringement is still infringement. A thoughtful infringement is still infringement. The law does not reward good intentions. It measures conduct and effect.

This is why fair use analysis feels so unsatisfying. It does not track how creators experience their own work.

The Only Question That Actually Matters

When the analysis is stripped down, fair use often collapses into a single practical inquiry:

Could this work stand on its own without the borrowed material?

If the answer is no, risk is high regardless of purpose, tone, or sincerity. Commentary does not save a work that depends on the underlying material to function. Transformation does not rescue a product that collapses when the original is removed.

This is not a legal test. It is a diagnostic creators can apply before publication and rarely do.

Dependency Is the Risk

Using third party material is not the problem. Depending on it is.

Most creators focus on amount. How much they took. How short the clip was. How little they showed. Courts focus on role.

If the audience came primarily for the borrowed work, if the borrowed work is the hook, if the borrowed work carries the value, then the creator has crossed from use into reliance.

Fair use does not fail because too much was copied. It fails because the copied material mattered too much.

When Fair Use Becomes Strategy

Fair use was never designed to support repeatable formats. It was designed to excuse specific uses under specific circumstances.

The moment fair use becomes a strategy, something planned, scaled, and repeated, exposure multiplies. "Play the Clip" formats, recurring segments built around borrowed material, monetization tied to third party works, and optimization for algorithmic performance all signal the same thing.

This is no longer incidental use. It is structural reliance.

Courts see that immediately, even when creators do not.

Why Legal Advice Sounds Like a Non-Answer

Creators want certainty. Lawyers offer probability.

That is not evasion. It is honesty.

Fair use cannot be approved in advance. It cannot be certified. It cannot be guaranteed. Courts decide after the fact, under circumstances the creator does not control.

Risk is assessed forward looking, but judgment is backward looking. That gap never closes.

Anyone promising certainty is selling comfort, not accuracy.

The Discipline Fair Use Actually Requires

Responsible fair use is not conservative. It is disciplined.

It requires restraint when something would clearly perform better. It requires discomfort when growth would be easier with borrowed material. It requires declining uses that could be justified but are not necessary.

That discipline rarely feels heroic. It often feels inconvenient. And it is invisible until it is not.

What This Book Has Actually Been About

This guide was never about winning fair use cases. It was about avoiding the need to explain yourself to a court at all.

Fair use is not protection. It is managed exposure.

Creators who understand that stop arguing from moral high ground and start making structural decisions. They do not ask whether they can justify a use. They ask whether they need it.

That shift does not make the work safer.

It makes the creator clearer.

And clarity, not confidence, is what survives scrutiny.

Chapter Twenty

THE DECISION HAPPENS BEFORE YOU PUBLISH

Every fair use case is decided after the fact.

By the time the analysis begins, copying has already occurred or is alleged to have occurred. The work is fixed. The record exists. The explanation no longer belongs to the creator.

That timing creates the central tension of fair use.

Courts evaluate uses backward, reconstructing decisions after publication. Creators make those decisions forward, under pressure, with incomplete information and no guarantee that the facts will later be interpreted the same way.

Most fair use disputes never reach a courtroom at all. They resolve earlier through takedown notices, demand letters, negotiated settlements, or quiet changes in behavior. Those outcomes rarely produce opinions, but they still impose cost and consequence. The absence of a litigated case does not mean the absence of exposure.

Fair use is judged backward.

Risk must be assessed forward.

Why Rules Fail at the Moment of Choice

Creators understandably look for rules. Bright lines. Checklists. Safe harbors. Something reliable enough to follow in the moment.

Fair use offers none of that.

It offers standards that depend on facts, context, markets, and effect. Those variables shift constantly. Formats evolve. Platforms change. Audiences migrate. What felt defensible at the moment of creation may look very different when reconstructed later.

Any checklist that promises certainty is offering reassurance, not accuracy.

What Creators Actually Control

At the moment of decision, creators control very little.

They do not control how a court will interpret the work.

They do not control how a rights holder will respond.

They do not control how markets or platforms will react.

They control something more demanding.

They control whether the borrowed material is necessary.

They control whether it is doing the work.

They control whether the audience could engage without it.

They control whether the format survives its removal.

Those questions do not require legal doctrine. They require honest self-reflection.

Restraint Is Not External Pressure

Restraint is often framed as something imposed from the outside. Platform rules. Legal threats. Audience backlash. Comment sections that rush to judgment and mistake outrage for authority.

That framing is misleading.

Restraint is not fear of consequences. It is authorship.

It is the decision to build a work that stands on its own terms. It is the choice to rely on original expression rather than borrowed gravity. It is the discipline to leave something out even when inclusion would clearly perform better.

Restraint Shapes the Record

Courts do not reward restraint directly. But restraint reshapes the facts courts eventually see.

It changes how a work functions.

It changes what role borrowed material plays.

It changes whether third party content appears incidental or essential.

That is not timidity. It is smart authorship.

As discussed in the interlude, creative decisions are made not only in what is included in a broadcast, but in what is excluded and why. Those decisions are invisible to audiences, but they are legible in hindsight.

When Judgment Replaces Justification

There is a point many creators reach, often quietly, where the analysis shifts.

They stop asking whether a use can be justified.

They start asking whether it should be used at all.

This does not eliminate the need for legal counsel. It improves it. The questions brought to lawyers become narrower, more concrete, and more strategic. Lawyers evaluate exposure. Creators decide what exposure is worth carrying.

Those roles do not replace one another. They align.

The Cost of Being Wrong Is Usually Friction

Fair use mistakes rarely destroy careers. They do something more subtle.

They introduce friction.

Takedowns. Disputes. Delay. Defensive posture. Time spent responding instead of creating. Opportunities lost while attention is diverted into explanation and repair.

Over time, that friction accumulates.

The Posture This Book Has Been Building

This guide was never meant to tell creators what they are allowed to do.

It was meant to help them see what they are actually doing, and how those choices look once stripped of intention, context, and explanation.

Fair use is not permission.

It is responsibility under uncertainty.

The decision that matters most is not the one a court makes years later. It is the one made quietly before publication, when no one is watching and no one is advising.

That is where clarity lives.

And clarity, not confidence, not cleverness, not justification, is what survives scrutiny.

EPILOGUE – WHAT YOU KNOW NOW

By the time you reach this page, something should feel different.
Not because you memorized rules.
Not because fair use suddenly feels safe.
But because you now understand where the risk actually lives.

Fair use did not become clearer because the doctrine changed. It became clearer because the illusions around it have been removed.

You know now that fair use is not permission.
You know it is not moral cover.
You know it is not something you "have" before you publish.

It is something argued later, by someone else, using a record you no longer control.

That understanding is uncomfortable. It should be.

Creators are often told to be confident. To trust their instincts. To move fast and fix things later. That advice works for growth. It works for platforms. It works for distribution.

It does not work for fair use.

What works instead is clarity.

Clarity about what you used.
Clarity about why you needed it.
Clarity about whether your work would survive without it.
Clarity about the role borrowed material actually plays.

Those questions do not disappear with experience. They sharpen.

Nothing in this book guarantees safety. That was never the point. What it offers is something more durable: the ability to see your own work the way a court will eventually see it, stripped of intention, stripped of explanation, reduced to function and effect.

Once you can do that, your decisions change.
Not because you are afraid.
Because you understand.

You will still take risks. You should. Creation requires it. But they will be conscious risks, not inherited habits. Chosen, not assumed.

That is the difference between confidence and competence.

Fair use does not reward cleverness, speed, or certainty. It rewards restraint when restraint reshapes the work, and independence when independence is possible.

If there is a single takeaway, it is this:

The most important fair use decision is not the one made by a judge years later. It is the one you make quietly, before publication, when no one is watching.

That is where authorship lives and responsibility begins.

And now, at least, you know where to look.

PROBLEM-DRIVEN INDEX

Start with your question, not the chapter.

COMMON MYTHS

"I gave credit, so I'm fine."

"It's only a short clip."

"I'm not making money from it."

"It's on the internet, so it's free to use."

"They haven't complained, so it must be okay."

None of these are legal defenses.

IF SOMETHING GOES WRONG

Read This Before You Do Anything Else

If you received a complaint, a takedown notice, or a message that made your stomach drop, stop.

Do not respond yet. Do not argue. Do not delete anything.

Start here:

1. Freeze the Situation

Before you touch anything, preserve it.
Take screenshots. Save the page. Copy the link. If it is audio or video, download the exact version that was published. You may not get another chance to capture what was actually out there.

2. Figure Out What You Are Being Accused Of

Not all problems are the same.
Is this copyright? Defamation? Something else?
If you misidentify the issue, you will respond the wrong way.

3. Ignore the Myths

This is where people make it worse.
Giving credit does not make it legal.
Using a short clip does not make it legal.
Not making money does not make it legal.
Those are talking points. Not defenses.

4. Do Not Litigate in Public

Do not jump on air. Do not post a thread. Do not "clarify" your intent.
Anything you say publicly becomes part of the situation.
And you do not control how it will be used later.

5. Decide — Don't React

You have three basic options:
Leave it up
Edit it
Take it down
Each one has consequences.

- Taking it down may reduce exposure, but it is not an admission.
- Leaving it up may be justified, but it carries risk.
- Make the decision deliberately. Not emotionally.

6. Understand What Actually Matters

The question is not what you meant.
The question is what you used, how you used it, and what effect it had.
That is what will be evaluated.

7. If It's Real, Get Help

If the complaint involves a real person, a company, or a formal demand, do not guess.
Get advice before you respond.
Because once you respond, you are in it.

8. Write Down Your Reasoning

Whatever you decide, write it down.
Why you used the material.
Why you kept it or removed it.

That record may matter later.

Final Thought
Most problems get worse because of the second move, not the first one.
Slow down. Think. *Then* act.

Made in United States
Orlando, FL
04 November 2026

90200944R00079